DON'T WORRY, BE CAPY

DON'T WORRY, BE CAPY

Fail-safe tips for living your best life from the world's friendliest giant rodent

Sarah Jackson

Published in 2026 by Dog 'n' Bone Books
An imprint of Ryland Peters & Small Ltd
20–21 Jockey's Fields, London WC1R 4BW
www.rylandpeters.com
Email: euregulations@rylandpeters.com

10 9 8 7 6 5 4 3 2 1

A CIP record for this book is available from the British Library.
US Library of Congress CIP data has been applied for.

ISBN: 978-1-912983-93-3

Printed in China

Assistant editor: Danielle Rawlings
Senior designer: Emily Breen
Art director: Sally Powell
Creative director: Leslie Harrington
Production manager: Gordana Simakovic
Publishing manager: Carmel Edmonds

The authorised representative in the EEA is
Authorised Rep Compliance Ltd.,
Ground Floor. 71 Lower Baggot Street,
Dublin, D01 P593, Ireland
www.arccompliance.com

CONTENTS

INTRODUCTION

Has anyone noticed that the world has gone a little crazy for capybaras lately?

Search "capybara" on social media and your screen will be filled with enough memes and capy-content to keep you entertained for hours. But what's with this recent phenomenon? Have some intrepid explorers discovered a fab new species?

Not so!
Here's a quick
history lesson
for you.

Capybaras have been roaming the earth for millions of years (circa 30–40 million BCE to be somewhat precise). That's not quite as old as dinosaurs, but it's well before the first human came into existence.
DINOSAURS 235–66 million years BCE
FISH 530 million years BCE

HUMANS
2.5 million
years BCE
CAPYBARAS
40 million
years BCE

Capybaras are definitely not the new kid on the block, but it certainly seems like they're having their moment. So why's everyone going wild for this chunky, oversized rodent? Let's take a minute to get to know this creature and see if we can work out what's got the world going capy-crazy.

CAPYBARA **FACTFILE**

Scientific name: *Hydrochoerus hydrochaeris* (what a tongue twister!)

Animal group: Rodent

Closest relative: Guinea pigs

Native to: South American wetlands

Size: Approximately the size of a Golden Retriever dog

Weight: Approx 75–150 lbs/34–68 kg (a. k. a. pretty heavy for a guinea pig)

HOW TO SPOT A CAPYBARA

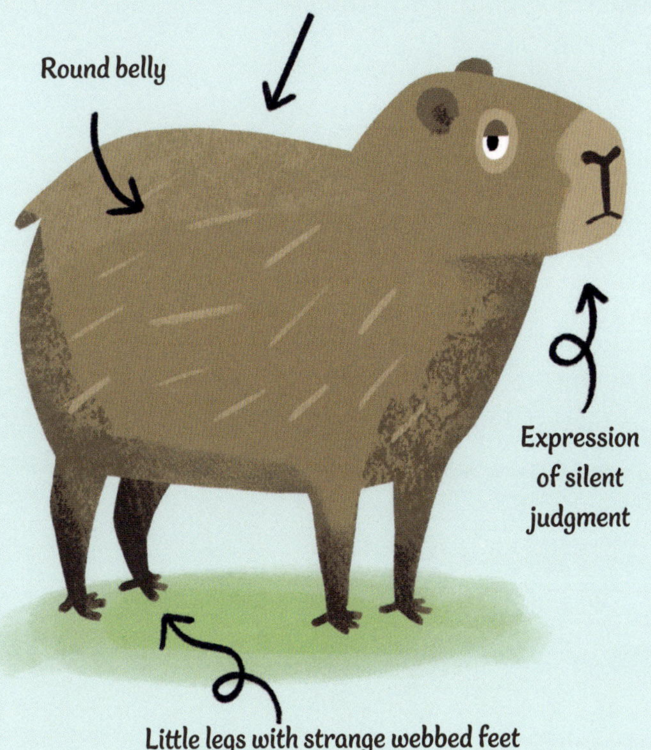

Okay, so you may be forgiven for thinking that the capybara is fairly uninteresting. Or, judging by that cold, hard stare, rather uninterested. By *everything*.

But we've been doing some research and the results are rather extraordinary. It turns out that the capybara's popularity is down to one very straightforward, undeniable fact...

BECAUSE THEY ARE FRICKIN' AWESOME!

Quick disclaimer:
This drawing is for illustration purposes only. Capybaras are definitely incapable of flight, even with a cape and an infinite amount of awesomeness.

If capybaras have been pottering around being amazing for 40 million years... we think it's about time that we learned a thing or two from them on how we can be more capy.

NESS

Let's discover the five pillars of capyness!

CHAPTER ONE

RELATIONSHIPS

COMMUNICATION

Communication is key to expressing your emotions and feeling heard and understood. Capybaras know the importance of choosing the right method of communication, which is why they have evolved to convey their feelings through an advanced range of styles.

TRANSLATIONS

WHISTLE: *Where are you?*

CLICK: *I'm enjoying your company.*

GRUNT: *You're getting on my nerves now.*

PARP: *I've eaten too much and you should probably vacate the area.*

FIND YOUR TRIBE

Capybaras are known for being a super social bunch and for having a big inner circle of friends and family—as well as a vast network of buddies, passerbys, and casual acquaintances of all shapes and sizes.

They are nature's socialites! And they love nothing more than getting up close and personal with their pals.

That's too close.

FUN FACT

DID YOU KNOW THAT IN JAPAN, CAPYBARAS ARE SO POPULAR THAT THEY HAVE CAPY CAFES? THAT'S RIGHT! YOU CAN COZY UP TO A CAPYBARA WHILE YOU CHOW DOWN ON A COFFEE AND YOUR FAVORITE PASTRY.

CAPY COFFEE CO.

FAMILY

Capybaras know the importance of family.

Family is everything. We stick together through thick and thin. We show each other respect and have a strong sense of loyalty. And most importantly, we pretend not to notice when someone toots in the hot tub.
(Yes, hot tubs—see page 58!)

KIDS

Anyone who has them knows that kids are a recipe for sleepless nights, elevated stress levels, and less time for relaxation. But not if you're a capybara—their motto is the more, the merrier! They love kids. The average capybara will have between 40–60 babies in their lifetime.

Humans: Don't try this at home! You will never be chilled enough to have that many kids.

ENEMIES

As we have already established, capybaras are loved by all. Sadly, some creatures love them for their full-bodied flavor rather than their charm and wit.

Come and
have a cuddle—
I want to give you
a good squeeze...

But capybaras are lovers, not fighters, and they will use their smarts to stay clear of danger!

CHAPTER TWO

DIET & NUTRITION

A HEALTHY DIET

Capybaras are herbivores. That means they eat a plant-based diet—also known as veganism, which has become very fashionable these days. Coincidence? We think not!

Little capybara joke for you...
Why don't capybaras ever argue?
Because they don't like beef!

TREATS

As much as a healthy diet is important, capybaras know it's good to allow yourself a little treat from time to time (every few hours).

After all, life's for living and having a good time. Allow yourself some of your favorite foods to make you feel good.

Can you guess what capybaras enjoy munching on as a little pudding after their main meal of grass and leaves?

Clue: It's brown and has a distinctive aroma...

That's right... CHOCOLATE!

Oh wait—that's not chocolate, is it? It's poop.

Capybaras practice coprophagy—the process of eating your own poop to make sure you get all of those important nutrients. Forget protein shakes and vitamin tablets—poop is the protein-packed superfood that keeps capybaras feeling so good!

Our advice:

Don't try this at home. Stick to the chocolate.

LETTING IT ALL OUT

*A little-known fact:
Capybaras are one of the most
flatulent animals around!*

*Well, all that vegetation and
nutrient-rich poop is bound to
make things a little bubbly.*

*But capybaras are not ones for
holding in unnecessary tension–
they've learned to let it all go...*

Inner capy-ness can be found through letting go. Let go of life's burdens and stresses... and more often than not, you'll let go of a little wind too.

CHAPTER THREE

EXERCISE & REST

STAYING ACTIVE

You've heard the saying "fit body, fit mind"? Well, it's true, my friends. Capybaras work hard(ish) to stay in peak physical condition, so they are equipped to deal with any life challenge that comes their way.

EXERCISE

It's important to find what works for you. If the gym isn't your thing... don't sweat it!

Capybaras may look like they are built for comfort rather than speed, so it may come as a surprise to hear that they can reach speeds of over 10 mph on land and swim as fast as an Olympic athlete!

However, due to their short legs and barrel-shaped bodies, there are a few sports that a capybara may struggle with...

Nope.

Also nope.

This is just
silly now.

WILD SWIMMING

This trendy human hobby has been practiced by capybaras since the dawn of time. The rush of cold water, the thrill of surrounding yourself with nature, the pondweed tickling your toes—now that's our kind of exercise!

FUN FACT

DID YOU KNOW THAT CAPYBARAS INVENTED SPAS?* THAT'S RIGHT! CAPYBARAS DISCOVERED THE ULTIMATE WAY TO CHILL BY TAKING A SOAK IN THE EARTH'S NATURAL THERMAL SPAS—WELL BEFORE THE ROMANS DID.

* Sort of. This fact remains unverified.

When in Rome, do as the Romans did!
Aren't we in Brazil?

MEDITATION

Exercise is important for maintaining a happy body, but capybaras know it's important to keep a happy mind, too. Try meditating. You don't need any specialist equipment or training—just find a comfy spot and stare vacantly into space for as long as possible, and you've pretty much nailed it.

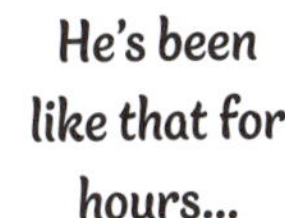
He's been like that for hours...
Have I got something on my face?

REST

All that exercise and socializing can be exhausting—even capybaras can drain their social batteries from time to time. It's important to make time for some R&R. So, put down your phone, turn on your out-of-office, and get some zzzs!

z
z
z
z
z

CHAPTER FOUR

HOME

LOCATION, LOCATION, LOCATION

It's important that you find the right spot to set up home—your environment needs to work for you, so make sure you factor this in when deciding where to live. Capybaras are pretty easy-going folk, but there are some settings that even they find hard to tolerate.

Too busy.

Too steep.

FUN FACT

DID YOU KNOW, CAPYBARAS ARE NATIVE TO EVERY COUNTRY IN SOUTH AMERICA, APART FROM CHILE?

FINDING YOUR HOME

They say "home is where the heart is" and they're not wrong.

Once you've found your perfect location, you need to find the right type of house.

It's perfect!

MAKE IT YOUR OWN

To really create a happy home, you need to make it your own. Anywhere can feel homely with some personal touches and a little bit of love. Here are some suggestions to get you going.

MISCELLANEOUS TRINKETS
Ornaments and foliage that make rooms look more interesting, even if they have no real purpose.

SENTIMENTAL ITEMS
Family photos, baby's first paw print, etc.

SOFT FURNISHINGS
Rugs, cushions, etc—a large palm leaf will often suffice.

ARTWORK

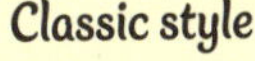

Classic style

Modern style

FUN FACT

DID YOU KNOW THAT CAPYBARAS ARE OFTEN REFERRED TO AS "NATURE'S COUCH"? WHY BLOW YOUR SAVINGS ON A FANCY DESIGNER SOFA WHEN YOU COULD JUST BEFRIEND A CAPYBARA? THESE WALKING BEANBAGS ARE SOFT, WARM, AND SLIGHTLY SQUEAKY... THEY'RE THE COMFIEST SOFA YOU'LL EVER FIND!

CHAPTER FIVE

POSITIVITY

CAN-DO ATTITUDE

Capybaras know that anything is possible when you adopt a can-do attitude. Even the most daunting task can be accomplished when you learn to take things in your stride.

Hop on my friend!

SMILE MORE

It's a proven fact that smiling makes you feel good. It doesn't come naturally for everyone but capybaras are blessed with some impressive gnashers that never stop growing. Get practicing; the more you try, the easier it becomes.

All the better for smiling with!

DON'T GET BOGGED DOWN BY LIFE

Sometimes, life can get the better of all of us, but it's important to keep some perspective and not let yourself get bogged down by the little things.*

* Metaphorically—it's best to avoid actual bogs, too.

GET LIFTED

Surround yourself with positivity. Ditch those "negative nellies" and spend time with those who lift you up (again, this is metaphorically speaking—no actual lifting is required most of the time).

BE YOUR OWN CHEERLEADER

You can't always rely on others to bring you joy, so it's good to be your own positivity ambassador. Remind yourself of how wonderful you are and how great life is by surrounding yourself with uplifting quotes.

BELIEVE IN YOURSELF
LIVE, LAUGH, LOVE
YOU'VE
GOT
THIS

DON'T BE JUDGMENTAL

Keep an open mind and try to refrain from making snap judgments about others. Everyone is entitled to their own opinions and to make their own life choices.

Just know that a capybara is always right.

I ♥
CAPYS

CONCLUSION

So there you have it. Capybaras, otherwise known as the best thing since sliced bread (although, if you've been paying attention, you'll know they've been around long before the invention of sliced bread). But, if you were ever unfamiliar with the almighty capybara, or unsure of this wonderful rodent's superpowers…

Consider yourself converted!

We can all benefit from being a little bit more capybara. Why not start today by welcoming some new pals into your life with a little capy-kindness and a warm, friendly attitude?

Or just book yourself into a spa.

ABOUT THE AUTHOR

Sarah Jackson is the illustrator behind the Stormy Knight greeting card brand, and has written and illustrated four books—*A Sloth's Guide to Taking it Easy*, *A Sloth's Guide to Etiquette*, *A Beginner's Guide to Goat Yoga*, and *No Drama Llama*, all published by Dog 'n' Bone. Sarah spends most of her time designing colorful contemporary greeting cards from her studio in Bristol, UK.